50 Small Batch Baking Recipes for Home

By: Kelly Johnson

Table of Contents

- Mini Chocolate Chip Cookies
- Single-Serve Brownie
- Raspberry Almond Scones
- Lemon Poppy Seed Muffins
- Small Batch Cinnamon Rolls
- Peanut Butter Blossoms
- Mini Cheesecakes
- Oatmeal Raisin Cookies
- Blueberry Crumble Bars
- Chocolate Mug Cake
- Mini Banana Bread
- Snickerdoodles
- Strawberry Shortcake Cups
- Mini Pumpkin Pies
- Single-Serve Apple Crisp
- Chocolate Chip Banana Muffins
- Peanut Butter Cup Cookies
- Mini Lemon Tarts
- Coconut Macaroons
- Small Batch Fudge
- Mini Pavlovas
- Carrot Cake Cupcakes
- Chocolate Espresso Cookies
- Mini Pound Cake
- Funfetti Cookies
- Small Batch Granola Bars
- Maple Pecan Muffins
- Mini Fruit Galettes
- Almond Joy Cookies
- Mini Key Lime Pies
- Brown Butter Chocolate Chip Cookies
- Small Batch Biscotti
- Mini Tiramisu
- Zucchini Bread Muffins
- Mini Chocolate Cupcakes

- Honey Lavender Shortbread
- Raspberry Cheesecake Bars
- Mini Whoopie Pies
- Chocolate-Dipped Biscotti
- Ginger Molasses Cookies
- Small Batch Sugar Cookies
- Mini Cornbread Muffins
- Lemon Blueberry Loaf
- Chocolate Swirl Muffins
- Mini Coconut Cream Pies
- Cherry Almond Crumb Bars
- Small Batch Brownies
- Chocolate Hazelnut Spread Cookies
- Mini Strawberry Rhubarb Crumble
- Vanilla Bean Cupcakes

Mini Chocolate Chip Cookies

Ingredients

- **½ cup** butter, softened
- **⅓ cup** brown sugar
- **⅓ cup** granulated sugar
- **1 large egg**
- **1 tsp** vanilla extract
- **1 ¼ cups** all-purpose flour
- **½ tsp** baking soda
- **¼ tsp** salt
- **½ cup** mini chocolate chips

Instructions

1. **Mix Wet Ingredients**: In a bowl, cream together butter, brown sugar, and granulated sugar. Add egg and vanilla, mixing well.
2. **Combine Dry Ingredients**: In another bowl, whisk flour, baking soda, and salt. Gradually add to the wet mixture, then stir in chocolate chips.
3. **Bake**: Drop spoonfuls onto a baking sheet and bake at 350°F (175°C) for 10-12 minutes until golden. Cool before serving.

Single-Serve Brownie

Ingredients

- **2 tbsp** butter, melted
- **2 tbsp** granulated sugar
- **1 tbsp** brown sugar
- **1 egg yolk**
- **1 tsp** vanilla extract
- **3 tbsp** all-purpose flour
- **2 tbsp** cocoa powder
- **Pinch of salt**

Instructions

1. **Mix Ingredients**: In a microwave-safe mug, combine melted butter, sugars, egg yolk, and vanilla. Stir until smooth.
2. **Add Dry Ingredients**: Mix in flour, cocoa powder, and salt until fully combined.
3. **Cook**: Microwave on high for 30-40 seconds. Let cool slightly before enjoying.

Raspberry Almond Scones

Ingredients

- **2 cups** all-purpose flour
- **¼ cup** sugar
- **1 tbsp** baking powder
- **½ tsp** salt
- **½ cup** cold butter, cubed
- **1 cup** fresh raspberries
- **½ cup** almond milk
- **1 tsp** almond extract
- **Egg wash** (optional)

Instructions

1. **Mix Dry Ingredients**: In a bowl, combine flour, sugar, baking powder, and salt. Cut in butter until the mixture resembles coarse crumbs.
2. **Combine Wet Ingredients**: Stir in raspberries, almond milk, and almond extract until just combined.
3. **Shape & Bake**: Turn onto a floured surface, shape into a circle, and cut into wedges. Place on a baking sheet and brush with egg wash if desired. Bake at 400°F (200°C) for 15-20 minutes until golden.

Lemon Poppy Seed Muffins

Ingredients

- **1 ½ cups** all-purpose flour
- **½ cup** sugar
- **1 tsp** baking powder
- **½ tsp** baking soda
- **¼ tsp** salt
- **1 large egg**
- **½ cup** milk
- **¼ cup** vegetable oil
- **1 tbsp** lemon zest
- **2 tbsp** poppy seeds

Instructions

1. **Mix Dry Ingredients**: In a bowl, combine flour, sugar, baking powder, baking soda, and salt.
2. **Combine Wet Ingredients**: In another bowl, whisk egg, milk, oil, lemon zest, and poppy seeds. Add to dry ingredients and mix until just combined.
3. **Bake**: Divide batter into muffin tins and bake at 350°F (175°C) for 18-20 minutes until a toothpick comes out clean.

Small Batch Cinnamon Rolls

Ingredients

- **1 cup** all-purpose flour
- **2 tbsp** sugar
- **½ tsp** baking powder
- **¼ tsp** baking soda
- **¼ tsp** salt
- **2 tbsp** butter, melted
- **½ cup** milk
- **2 tbsp** cinnamon
- **2 tbsp** brown sugar

Instructions

1. **Make Dough**: In a bowl, mix flour, sugar, baking powder, baking soda, and salt. Stir in melted butter and milk until combined.
2. **Roll Out**: On a floured surface, roll the dough into a rectangle. Sprinkle with cinnamon and brown sugar, then roll up tightly.
3. **Bake**: Cut into rolls and place in a baking dish. Bake at 375°F (190°C) for 15-20 minutes until golden.

Peanut Butter Blossoms

Ingredients

- **½ cup** peanut butter
- **⅓ cup** sugar
- **⅓ cup** brown sugar
- **1 large egg**
- **½ tsp** vanilla extract
- **½ tsp** baking soda
- **¼ tsp** salt
- **12 chocolate kisses**

Instructions

1. **Mix Ingredients**: In a bowl, combine peanut butter, sugars, egg, vanilla, baking soda, and salt until smooth.
2. **Form Cookies**: Roll into balls and place on a baking sheet. Bake at 350°F (175°C) for 8-10 minutes.
3. **Add Kisses**: Immediately press a chocolate kiss into the center of each cookie after baking. Cool before serving.

Mini Cheesecakes

Ingredients

- **1 cup** cream cheese, softened
- **⅓ cup** sugar
- **1 tsp** vanilla extract
- **1 large egg**
- **Graham cracker crumbs** (for crust)
- **Fruit topping** (optional)

Instructions

1. **Prepare Crust**: Mix graham cracker crumbs with a bit of melted butter and press into the bottom of muffin tins.
2. **Make Filling**: In a bowl, beat cream cheese, sugar, vanilla, and egg until smooth. Pour over the crust.
3. **Bake**: Bake at 325°F (160°C) for 20-25 minutes. Cool and top with fruit before serving.

Oatmeal Raisin Cookies

Ingredients

- **½ cup** butter, softened
- **¾ cup** brown sugar
- **¼ cup** granulated sugar
- **1 large egg**
- **1 tsp** vanilla extract
- **1 cup** all-purpose flour
- **½ tsp** baking soda
- **½ tsp** cinnamon
- **1 ½ cups** rolled oats
- **½ cup** raisins

Instructions

1. **Mix Wet Ingredients**: In a bowl, cream together butter, brown sugar, and granulated sugar. Add egg and vanilla, mixing well.
2. **Combine Dry Ingredients**: In another bowl, whisk flour, baking soda, and cinnamon. Gradually add to the wet mixture, then stir in oats and raisins.
3. **Bake**: Drop spoonfuls onto a baking sheet and bake at 350°F (175°C) for 10-12 minutes until golden. Cool before serving.

Enjoy these delicious treats!

Blueberry Crumble Bars

Ingredients

- 1 ½ **cups** all-purpose flour
- ¾ **cup** oats
- ½ **cup** brown sugar
- ½ **cup** butter, softened
- 2 **cups** fresh blueberries
- ¼ **cup** sugar
- 1 **tbsp** lemon juice
- 1 **tbsp** cornstarch
- ½ **tsp** cinnamon

Instructions

1. **Prepare Crust**: In a bowl, mix flour, oats, brown sugar, and butter until crumbly. Press half into the bottom of a greased baking dish.
2. **Make Filling**: In another bowl, combine blueberries, sugar, lemon juice, cornstarch, and cinnamon. Pour over the crust.
3. **Add Crumble Topping**: Sprinkle remaining crumble on top. Bake at 350°F (175°C) for 25-30 minutes. Cool before slicing.

Chocolate Mug Cake

Ingredients

- **4 tbsp** all-purpose flour
- **4 tbsp** granulated sugar
- **2 tbsp** cocoa powder
- **1/8 tsp** baking powder
- **Pinch of salt**
- **3 tbsp** milk
- **2 tbsp** vegetable oil
- **1/4 tsp** vanilla extract

Instructions

1. **Mix Dry Ingredients**: In a microwave-safe mug, whisk together flour, sugar, cocoa powder, baking powder, and salt.
2. **Add Wet Ingredients**: Stir in milk, vegetable oil, and vanilla until smooth.
3. **Cook**: Microwave on high for 1 minute and 30 seconds. Let cool slightly before enjoying.

Mini Banana Bread

Ingredients

- **1 ripe banana**, mashed
- **1/4 cup** sugar
- **1 egg**
- **1/4 cup** butter, melted
- **1 tsp** vanilla extract
- **1 cup** all-purpose flour
- **1/2 tsp** baking soda
- **1/4 tsp** salt

Instructions

1. **Mix Wet Ingredients**: In a bowl, combine mashed banana, sugar, egg, melted butter, and vanilla.
2. **Add Dry Ingredients**: Stir in flour, baking soda, and salt until just combined.
3. **Bake**: Pour into a greased mini loaf pan and bake at 350°F (175°C) for 25-30 minutes. Cool before slicing.

Snickerdoodles

Ingredients

- **½ cup** butter, softened
- **¾ cup** sugar
- **1 large egg**
- **1 tsp** vanilla extract
- **1 ½ cups** all-purpose flour
- **½ tsp** baking soda
- **½ tsp** cream of tartar
- **¼ tsp** salt
- **2 tbsp** sugar (for coating)
- **1 tsp** cinnamon (for coating)

Instructions

1. **Mix Wet Ingredients**: In a bowl, cream together butter and sugar. Add egg and vanilla, mixing well.
2. **Combine Dry Ingredients**: In another bowl, whisk flour, baking soda, cream of tartar, and salt. Gradually add to the wet mixture.
3. **Shape Cookies**: Roll into balls, then coat in a mixture of sugar and cinnamon. Bake at 350°F (175°C) for 8-10 minutes. Cool before serving.

Strawberry Shortcake Cups

Ingredients

- **1 cup** strawberries, sliced
- **2 tbsp** sugar
- **1 cup** whipped cream
- **1 cup** biscuit or cake, crumbled (store-bought or homemade)

Instructions

1. **Prepare Strawberries**: Toss sliced strawberries with sugar and let sit for 10 minutes.
2. **Assemble Cups**: In small cups, layer crumbled biscuit or cake, strawberries, and whipped cream.
3. **Serve**: Repeat layers and serve immediately.

Mini Pumpkin Pies

Ingredients

- **1 cup** pumpkin puree
- **½ cup** sugar
- **1 tsp** cinnamon
- **¼ tsp** nutmeg
- **¼ tsp** ginger
- **1 large egg**
- **½ cup** evaporated milk
- **Mini pie crusts** (store-bought or homemade)

Instructions

1. **Mix Filling**: In a bowl, combine pumpkin puree, sugar, spices, egg, and evaporated milk until smooth.
2. **Fill Crusts**: Pour filling into mini pie crusts.
3. **Bake**: Bake at 350°F (175°C) for 25-30 minutes until set. Cool before serving.

Single-Serve Apple Crisp

Ingredients

- **1 small apple**, diced
- **1 tbsp** sugar
- **½ tsp** cinnamon
- **2 tbsp** oats
- **1 tbsp** flour
- **1 tbsp** butter, softened

Instructions

1. **Prepare Filling**: In a small bowl, toss diced apple with sugar and cinnamon. Place in a microwave-safe dish.
2. **Make Topping**: In another bowl, mix oats, flour, and butter until crumbly. Sprinkle over the apples.
3. **Cook**: Microwave for 2-3 minutes until apples are tender. Serve warm.

Chocolate Chip Banana Muffins

Ingredients

- **1 ripe banana**, mashed
- **1/3 cup** sugar
- **1 large egg**
- **1/4 cup** melted butter
- **1 tsp** vanilla extract
- **1 cup** all-purpose flour
- **1/2 tsp** baking soda
- **1/2 tsp** baking powder
- **1/4 tsp** salt
- **1/2 cup** chocolate chips

Instructions

1. **Mix Wet Ingredients**: In a bowl, combine mashed banana, sugar, egg, melted butter, and vanilla.
2. **Add Dry Ingredients**: Stir in flour, baking soda, baking powder, and salt until just combined. Fold in chocolate chips.
3. **Bake**: Pour into muffin tins and bake at 350°F (175°C) for 15-20 minutes until a toothpick comes out clean.

Enjoy these delicious treats!

Peanut Butter Cup Cookies

Ingredients

- ½ **cup** peanut butter
- ½ **cup** butter, softened
- ¾ **cup** brown sugar
- ½ **cup** granulated sugar
- **1 large egg**
- **1 tsp** vanilla extract
- **1 ½ cups** all-purpose flour
- **½ tsp** baking soda
- **¼ tsp** salt
- **12 mini peanut butter cups**, unwrapped

Instructions

1. **Mix Wet Ingredients**: In a bowl, cream together peanut butter, butter, brown sugar, and granulated sugar. Add egg and vanilla, mixing well.
2. **Combine Dry Ingredients**: In another bowl, whisk flour, baking soda, and salt. Gradually add to the wet mixture.
3. **Bake**: Roll dough into balls and place on a baking sheet. Bake at 350°F (175°C) for 8-10 minutes. Immediately press a peanut butter cup into each cookie. Cool before serving.

Mini Lemon Tarts

Ingredients

- **1 cup** all-purpose flour
- **½ cup** unsalted butter, softened
- **¼ cup** powdered sugar
- **1 egg**
- **½ cup** fresh lemon juice
- **½ cup** granulated sugar
- **1 tsp** lemon zest
- **1 tsp** cornstarch

Instructions

1. **Make Crust**: In a bowl, combine flour, butter, and powdered sugar until crumbly. Press into mini tart pans.
2. **Prepare Filling**: In another bowl, whisk egg, lemon juice, granulated sugar, lemon zest, and cornstarch until smooth. Pour into crusts.
3. **Bake**: Bake at 350°F (175°C) for 15-20 minutes until set. Cool before serving.

Coconut Macaroons

Ingredients

- **2 ¾ cups** shredded coconut
- **⅓ cup** sugar
- **¼ cup** all-purpose flour
- **¼ tsp** salt
- **2 large egg whites**
- **1 tsp** vanilla extract
- **½ cup** chocolate chips (optional, for drizzling)

Instructions

1. **Mix Ingredients**: In a bowl, combine shredded coconut, sugar, flour, salt, egg whites, and vanilla until well mixed.
2. **Form Macaroons**: Scoop tablespoon-sized mounds onto a baking sheet.
3. **Bake**: Bake at 325°F (160°C) for 15-20 minutes until golden. Drizzle with melted chocolate if desired.

Small Batch Fudge

Ingredients

- **1 cup** chocolate chips
- **1 can (14 oz)** sweetened condensed milk
- **1 tsp** vanilla extract
- **Pinch of salt**

Instructions

1. **Melt Ingredients**: In a saucepan, combine chocolate chips, sweetened condensed milk, vanilla, and salt. Cook over low heat until melted and smooth.
2. **Set Fudge**: Pour into a lined small baking dish and refrigerate for 2-3 hours until set. Cut into squares before serving.

Mini Pavlovas

Ingredients

- **2 large egg whites**
- **½ cup** granulated sugar
- **1 tsp** cornstarch
- **1 tsp** white vinegar
- **1 tsp** vanilla extract
- **Whipped cream** and **fresh fruit** for topping

Instructions

1. **Preheat Oven**: Preheat oven to 250°F (120°C).
2. **Whip Egg Whites**: In a bowl, whip egg whites until soft peaks form. Gradually add sugar until glossy. Fold in cornstarch, vinegar, and vanilla.
3. **Shape and Bake**: Spoon mounds onto a baking sheet. Bake for 1 hour, then turn off the oven and let cool inside. Top with whipped cream and fruit before serving.

Carrot Cake Cupcakes

Ingredients

- **1 cup** all-purpose flour
- **½ tsp** baking soda
- **½ tsp** baking powder
- **¼ tsp** salt
- **½ tsp** cinnamon
- **½ cup** sugar
- **½ cup** vegetable oil
- **1 large egg**
- **1 cup** grated carrots
- **½ cup** chopped walnuts (optional)

Instructions

1. **Mix Dry Ingredients**: In a bowl, whisk flour, baking soda, baking powder, salt, and cinnamon.
2. **Combine Wet Ingredients**: In another bowl, mix sugar, oil, and egg. Stir in grated carrots and walnuts.
3. **Combine & Bake**: Gradually add dry ingredients to wet. Pour into cupcake liners and bake at 350°F (175°C) for 15-20 minutes. Cool before frosting.

Chocolate Espresso Cookies

Ingredients

- **½ cup** butter, softened
- **¾ cup** sugar
- **1 large egg**
- **1 tsp** vanilla extract
- **1 cup** all-purpose flour
- **¼ cup** cocoa powder
- **½ tsp** baking soda
- **¼ cup** espresso powder
- **½ cup** chocolate chips

Instructions

1. **Mix Wet Ingredients**: In a bowl, cream together butter and sugar. Add egg and vanilla, mixing well.
2. **Combine Dry Ingredients**: In another bowl, whisk flour, cocoa powder, baking soda, and espresso powder. Gradually add to the wet mixture. Stir in chocolate chips.
3. **Bake**: Drop spoonfuls onto a baking sheet and bake at 350°F (175°C) for 10-12 minutes. Cool before serving.

Mini Pound Cake

Ingredients

- **½ cup** butter, softened
- **¾ cup** sugar
- **2 large eggs**
- **1 tsp** vanilla extract
- **1 cup** all-purpose flour
- **¼ tsp** baking powder
- **Pinch of salt**

Instructions

1. **Mix Wet Ingredients**: In a bowl, cream together butter and sugar. Add eggs and vanilla, mixing well.
2. **Combine Dry Ingredients**: In another bowl, whisk flour, baking powder, and salt. Gradually add to the wet mixture.
3. **Bake**: Pour into a mini loaf pan and bake at 350°F (175°C) for 30-35 minutes. Cool before slicing.

Enjoy these delightful treats!

Funfetti Cookies

Ingredients

- **½ cup** butter, softened
- **¾ cup** sugar
- **1 large egg**
- **1 tsp** vanilla extract
- **1 ½ cups** all-purpose flour
- **½ tsp** baking powder
- **¼ tsp** salt
- **¼ cup** rainbow sprinkles

Instructions

1. **Mix Wet Ingredients**: In a bowl, cream together butter and sugar. Add egg and vanilla, mixing well.
2. **Combine Dry Ingredients**: In another bowl, whisk flour, baking powder, and salt. Gradually add to the wet mixture. Stir in sprinkles.
3. **Bake**: Drop spoonfuls onto a baking sheet and bake at 350°F (175°C) for 10-12 minutes. Cool before serving.

Small Batch Granola Bars

Ingredients

- **1 cup** rolled oats
- **¼ cup** honey or maple syrup
- **¼ cup** nut butter (peanut or almond)
- **¼ cup** nuts or seeds (chopped)
- **¼ cup** dried fruit (chopped)

Instructions

1. **Mix Ingredients**: In a bowl, combine oats, honey, nut butter, nuts, and dried fruit until well mixed.
2. **Press into Pan**: Spread mixture into a lined small baking dish, pressing down firmly.
3. **Chill & Cut**: Refrigerate for at least 1 hour, then cut into bars.

Maple Pecan Muffins

Ingredients

- **1 cup** all-purpose flour
- **½ cup** chopped pecans
- **½ cup** maple syrup
- **1 large egg**
- **¼ cup** milk
- **¼ cup** butter, melted
- **½ tsp** baking powder
- **¼ tsp** baking soda
- **¼ tsp** salt

Instructions

1. **Mix Wet Ingredients**: In a bowl, combine maple syrup, egg, milk, and melted butter.
2. **Combine Dry Ingredients**: In another bowl, whisk flour, baking powder, baking soda, salt, and pecans. Gradually add to wet ingredients.
3. **Bake**: Pour into muffin tins and bake at 350°F (175°C) for 15-20 minutes. Cool before serving.

Mini Fruit Galettes

Ingredients

- **1 cup** all-purpose flour
- **½ tsp** salt
- **½ cup** butter, chilled and cubed
- **3-4 tbsp** ice water
- **1 cup** mixed fresh fruit (berries, peaches, etc.)
- **2 tbsp** sugar

Instructions

1. **Make Dough**: In a bowl, mix flour and salt. Cut in butter until crumbly. Stir in ice water until dough forms. Chill for 30 minutes.
2. **Assemble Galettes**: Roll out dough and place on a baking sheet. Top with fruit and sprinkle with sugar. Fold edges over fruit.
3. **Bake**: Bake at 375°F (190°C) for 20-25 minutes until golden. Cool before serving.

Almond Joy Cookies

Ingredients

- **½ cup** butter, softened
- **¾ cup** sugar
- **1 large egg**
- **1 tsp** vanilla extract
- **1 cup** all-purpose flour
- **½ cup** shredded coconut
- **½ cup** chocolate chips
- **¼ cup** chopped almonds

Instructions

1. **Mix Wet Ingredients**: In a bowl, cream together butter and sugar. Add egg and vanilla, mixing well.
2. **Combine Dry Ingredients**: In another bowl, whisk flour, coconut, chocolate chips, and almonds. Gradually add to the wet mixture.
3. **Bake**: Drop spoonfuls onto a baking sheet and bake at 350°F (175°C) for 10-12 minutes. Cool before serving.

Mini Key Lime Pies

Ingredients

- **½ cup** graham cracker crumbs
- **¼ cup** sugar
- **¼ cup** butter, melted
- **1 egg**
- **½ cup** sweetened condensed milk
- **¼ cup** key lime juice
- **Zest of 1 lime**

Instructions

1. **Make Crust**: In a bowl, mix graham cracker crumbs, sugar, and melted butter. Press into mini tart pans.
2. **Prepare Filling**: In another bowl, whisk egg, condensed milk, lime juice, and zest until smooth. Pour into crusts.
3. **Bake**: Bake at 350°F (175°C) for 10-12 minutes. Cool before serving.

Brown Butter Chocolate Chip Cookies

Ingredients

- **½ cup** butter
- **¾ cup** brown sugar
- **¼ cup** granulated sugar
- **1 large egg**
- **1 tsp** vanilla extract
- **1 ½ cups** all-purpose flour
- **½ tsp** baking soda
- **¼ tsp** salt
- **½ cup** chocolate chips

Instructions

1. **Brown the Butter**: In a saucepan, melt butter over medium heat until browned. Let cool slightly.
2. **Mix Wet Ingredients**: In a bowl, combine browned butter, brown sugar, and granulated sugar. Add egg and vanilla, mixing well.
3. **Combine Dry Ingredients**: In another bowl, whisk flour, baking soda, and salt. Gradually add to the wet mixture. Stir in chocolate chips.
4. **Bake**: Drop spoonfuls onto a baking sheet and bake at 350°F (175°C) for 10-12 minutes. Cool before serving.

Small Batch Biscotti

Ingredients

- **½ cup** all-purpose flour
- **¼ cup** sugar
- **1 large egg**
- **¼ tsp** baking powder
- **¼ tsp** almond extract
- **¼ cup** chopped nuts (optional)

Instructions

1. **Mix Ingredients**: In a bowl, combine flour, sugar, egg, baking powder, and almond extract until a dough forms. Fold in nuts if using.
2. **Shape & Bake**: Form into a log on a baking sheet. Bake at 350°F (175°C) for 25 minutes. Cool slightly, then slice into biscotti shapes.
3. **Second Bake**: Return to the oven and bake for an additional 10-15 minutes until crisp. Cool before serving.

Enjoy these delightful treats!

Mini Tiramisu

Ingredients

- **1 cup** brewed coffee, cooled
- **2 tbsp** coffee liqueur (optional)
- **1 cup** mascarpone cheese
- **½ cup** heavy cream
- **¼ cup** sugar
- **1 tsp** vanilla extract
- **24 ladyfingers**
- **Cocoa powder** for dusting

Instructions

1. **Mix Coffee**: In a shallow dish, combine brewed coffee and coffee liqueur.
2. **Prepare Filling**: In a bowl, whip heavy cream with sugar and vanilla until soft peaks form. Gently fold in mascarpone.
3. **Assemble Tiramisu**: Dip ladyfingers in coffee mixture, then layer in small cups. Add a layer of mascarpone mixture. Repeat layers and dust with cocoa powder. Chill for 2 hours before serving.

Zucchini Bread Muffins

Ingredients

- **1 cup** grated zucchini
- **1 cup** all-purpose flour
- **½ cup** sugar
- **¼ cup** vegetable oil
- **1 large egg**
- **½ tsp** baking powder
- **½ tsp** baking soda
- **¼ tsp** salt
- **½ tsp** cinnamon

Instructions

1. **Mix Wet Ingredients**: In a bowl, combine grated zucchini, sugar, oil, and egg.
2. **Combine Dry Ingredients**: In another bowl, whisk flour, baking powder, baking soda, salt, and cinnamon. Gradually add to wet ingredients.
3. **Bake**: Pour into muffin tins and bake at 350°F (175°C) for 18-20 minutes. Cool before serving.

Mini Chocolate Cupcakes

Ingredients

- **½ cup** all-purpose flour
- **⅓ cup** cocoa powder
- **½ tsp** baking powder
- **¼ tsp** baking soda
- **¼ tsp** salt
- **½ cup** sugar
- **⅓ cup** vegetable oil
- **1 large egg**
- **½ tsp** vanilla extract
- **½ cup** water

Instructions

1. **Mix Dry Ingredients**: In a bowl, whisk flour, cocoa powder, baking powder, baking soda, salt, and sugar.
2. **Add Wet Ingredients**: Stir in oil, egg, vanilla, and water until smooth.
3. **Bake**: Pour into mini cupcake liners and bake at 350°F (175°C) for 10-12 minutes. Cool before frosting.

Honey Lavender Shortbread

Ingredients

- **1 cup** unsalted butter, softened
- **½ cup** sugar
- **2 cups** all-purpose flour
- **1 tbsp** dried lavender
- **2 tbsp** honey
- **¼ tsp** salt

Instructions

1. **Mix Ingredients**: In a bowl, cream together butter and sugar. Mix in honey, lavender, and salt. Gradually add flour until combined.
2. **Chill Dough**: Shape into a log, wrap in plastic, and chill for 1 hour.
3. **Bake**: Slice and place on a baking sheet. Bake at 350°F (175°C) for 12-15 minutes until lightly golden. Cool before serving.

Raspberry Cheesecake Bars

Ingredients

- **1 cup** graham cracker crumbs
- **¼ cup** sugar
- **½ cup** butter, melted
- **8 oz** cream cheese, softened
- **¼ cup** sugar
- **1 egg**
- **1 tsp** vanilla extract
- **½ cup** raspberry preserves

Instructions

1. **Prepare Crust**: Mix graham cracker crumbs, sugar, and melted butter. Press into a lined baking dish.
2. **Make Filling**: In a bowl, beat cream cheese with sugar, egg, and vanilla until smooth. Pour over crust and drop spoonfuls of raspberry preserves on top.
3. **Bake**: Bake at 350°F (175°C) for 25-30 minutes. Cool before slicing into bars.

Mini Whoopie Pies

Ingredients

- **½ cup** cocoa powder
- **1 cup** all-purpose flour
- **½ tsp** baking soda
- **½ tsp** baking powder
- **¼ tsp** salt
- **½ cup** butter, softened
- **½ cup** sugar
- **1 large egg**
- **½ cup** milk
- **1 tsp** vanilla extract
- **Filling**: 1 cup marshmallow fluff, ¼ cup butter, and ½ cup powdered sugar

Instructions

1. **Make Cookies**: In a bowl, whisk cocoa, flour, baking soda, baking powder, and salt. In another bowl, cream butter and sugar. Add egg, milk, and vanilla. Gradually add dry ingredients. Drop spoonfuls onto a baking sheet.
2. **Bake**: Bake at 350°F (175°C) for 10-12 minutes. Cool completely.
3. **Make Filling**: Beat marshmallow fluff, butter, and powdered sugar until smooth. Sandwich filling between two cookies.

Chocolate-Dipped Biscotti

Ingredients

- **1 cup** all-purpose flour
- **½ cup** sugar
- **½ tsp** baking powder
- **¼ tsp** salt
- **2 large eggs**
- **½ cup** almonds (or nuts of choice)
- **½ cup** chocolate chips (for dipping)

Instructions

1. **Mix Dry Ingredients**: In a bowl, whisk flour, sugar, baking powder, and salt. In another bowl, beat eggs. Gradually combine with dry ingredients and fold in almonds.
2. **Shape & Bake**: Shape into a log on a baking sheet. Bake at 350°F (175°C) for 25 minutes. Cool slightly, then slice into biscotti shapes.
3. **Second Bake**: Return to the oven and bake for another 10 minutes. Cool completely. Melt chocolate and dip biscotti ends.

Ginger Molasses Cookies

Ingredients

- **½ cup** unsalted butter, softened
- **½ cup** sugar
- **½ cup** molasses
- **1 large egg**
- **2 cups** all-purpose flour
- **1 tsp** baking soda
- **2 tsp** ground ginger
- **1 tsp** cinnamon
- **¼ tsp** salt
- **¼ cup** sugar (for rolling)

Instructions

1. **Mix Wet Ingredients**: In a bowl, cream together butter, sugar, and molasses. Beat in the egg.
2. **Combine Dry Ingredients**: In another bowl, whisk flour, baking soda, ginger, cinnamon, and salt. Gradually add to the wet mixture.
3. **Shape & Bake**: Roll into balls and coat in sugar. Bake at 350°F (175°C) for 10-12 minutes. Cool before serving.

Enjoy these delicious treats!

Small Batch Sugar Cookies

Ingredients

- **½ cup** unsalted butter, softened
- **½ cup** granulated sugar
- **1 large egg**
- **1 tsp** vanilla extract
- **1 ½ cups** all-purpose flour
- **½ tsp** baking powder
- **¼ tsp** salt

Instructions

1. **Mix Wet Ingredients**: In a bowl, cream together butter and sugar. Add egg and vanilla, mixing well.
2. **Combine Dry Ingredients**: In another bowl, whisk flour, baking powder, and salt. Gradually add to the wet mixture.
3. **Bake**: Roll into balls, place on a baking sheet, and flatten slightly. Bake at 350°F (175°C) for 10-12 minutes. Cool before serving.

Mini Cornbread Muffins

Ingredients

- **½ cup** cornmeal
- **½ cup** all-purpose flour
- **¼ cup** sugar
- **1 tsp** baking powder
- **¼ tsp** baking soda
- **¼ tsp** salt
- **1 large egg**
- **¾ cup** buttermilk
- **¼ cup** unsalted butter, melted

Instructions

1. **Mix Dry Ingredients**: In a bowl, whisk together cornmeal, flour, sugar, baking powder, baking soda, and salt.
2. **Combine Wet Ingredients**: In another bowl, mix egg, buttermilk, and melted butter. Combine with dry ingredients until just mixed.
3. **Bake**: Pour into mini muffin tins and bake at 400°F (200°C) for 10-12 minutes. Cool before serving.

Lemon Blueberry Loaf

Ingredients

- **1 cup** all-purpose flour
- **½ tsp** baking powder
- **¼ tsp** baking soda
- **¼ tsp** salt
- **¼ cup** unsalted butter, softened
- **½ cup** sugar
- **1 large egg**
- **¼ cup** sour cream
- **2 tbsp** lemon juice
- **1 tsp** lemon zest
- **½ cup** blueberries (fresh or frozen)

Instructions

1. **Mix Dry Ingredients**: In a bowl, whisk flour, baking powder, baking soda, and salt.
2. **Cream Butter and Sugar**: In another bowl, cream together butter and sugar. Add egg, sour cream, lemon juice, and zest, mixing well.
3. **Combine & Bake**: Gradually add dry ingredients and fold in blueberries. Pour into a greased loaf pan and bake at 350°F (175°C) for 50-60 minutes. Cool before slicing.

Chocolate Swirl Muffins

Ingredients

- **½ cup** all-purpose flour
- **¼ cup** cocoa powder
- **½ tsp** baking powder
- **¼ tsp** baking soda
- **¼ tsp** salt
- **¼ cup** sugar
- **¼ cup** milk
- **¼ cup** vegetable oil
- **1 large egg**
- **¼ cup** chocolate chips

Instructions

1. **Mix Dry Ingredients**: In a bowl, whisk together flour, cocoa powder, baking powder, baking soda, salt, and sugar.
2. **Combine Wet Ingredients**: In another bowl, mix milk, oil, and egg. Gradually combine with dry ingredients, then fold in chocolate chips.
3. **Bake**: Pour into muffin tins and swirl with a spoon. Bake at 350°F (175°C) for 15-18 minutes. Cool before serving.

Mini Coconut Cream Pies

Ingredients

- ½ **cup** graham cracker crumbs
- ¼ **cup** sugar
- ¼ **cup** butter, melted
- 1 **cup** coconut milk
- 1 **egg yolk**
- ¼ **cup** sugar
- 1 **tbsp** cornstarch
- 1 **tsp** vanilla extract
- ½ **cup** shredded coconut (toasted)

Instructions

1. **Make Crust**: Mix graham cracker crumbs, sugar, and melted butter. Press into mini tart pans.
2. **Prepare Filling**: In a saucepan, combine coconut milk, egg yolk, sugar, cornstarch, and vanilla. Cook over medium heat until thickened. Stir in shredded coconut.
3. **Assemble & Bake**: Pour filling into crusts and bake at 350°F (175°C) for 15-20 minutes. Cool before serving.

Cherry Almond Crumb Bars

Ingredients

- **1 cup** all-purpose flour
- **½ cup** rolled oats
- **½ cup** sugar
- **½ cup** butter, softened
- **½ cup** cherry preserves
- **½ tsp** almond extract
- **¼ tsp** salt

Instructions

1. **Make Crust**: In a bowl, mix flour, oats, sugar, and salt. Cut in butter until crumbly. Reserve ½ cup for topping.
2. **Assemble Bars**: Press remaining mixture into a lined baking dish. Spread cherry preserves on top and sprinkle reserved crumb mixture.
3. **Bake**: Bake at 350°F (175°C) for 25-30 minutes. Cool before slicing into bars.

Small Batch Brownies

Ingredients

- ¼ **cup** unsalted butter, melted
- ½ **cup** sugar
- **1 large egg**
- ¼ **tsp** vanilla extract
- ⅓ **cup** all-purpose flour
- ¼ **cup** cocoa powder
- ¼ **tsp** salt

Instructions

1. **Mix Ingredients**: In a bowl, mix melted butter and sugar. Add egg and vanilla, then stir in flour, cocoa powder, and salt until combined.
2. **Bake**: Pour into a greased small baking dish and bake at 350°F (175°C) for 20-25 minutes. Cool before cutting into squares.

Chocolate Hazelnut Spread Cookies

Ingredients

- **½ cup** butter, softened
- **⅓ cup** sugar
- **⅓ cup** brown sugar
- **1 large egg**
- **½ tsp** vanilla extract
- **1 ½ cups** all-purpose flour
- **½ tsp** baking soda
- **¼ tsp** salt
- **½ cup** chocolate hazelnut spread

Instructions

1. **Mix Wet Ingredients**: In a bowl, cream together butter, sugar, and brown sugar. Add egg and vanilla, mixing well.
2. **Combine Dry Ingredients**: In another bowl, whisk flour, baking soda, and salt. Gradually add to the wet mixture.
3. **Add Spread**: Stir in chocolate hazelnut spread until just combined.
4. **Bake**: Drop spoonfuls onto a baking sheet and bake at 350°F (175°C) for 10-12 minutes. Cool before serving.

Enjoy these delicious treats!

Mini Strawberry Rhubarb Crumble

Ingredients

- **1 cup** diced strawberries
- **1 cup** diced rhubarb
- **¼ cup** sugar
- **1 tbsp** cornstarch
- **1 tsp** vanilla extract
- **½ cup** rolled oats
- **½ cup** all-purpose flour
- **¼ cup** brown sugar
- **¼ cup** butter, melted

Instructions

1. **Preheat Oven**: Preheat to 350°F (175°C).
2. **Prepare Filling**: In a bowl, mix strawberries, rhubarb, sugar, cornstarch, and vanilla. Divide into mini baking dishes.
3. **Make Crumble Topping**: In another bowl, combine oats, flour, brown sugar, and melted butter. Mix until crumbly.
4. **Assemble and Bake**: Sprinkle crumble topping over fruit. Bake for 25-30 minutes until bubbly and golden. Cool slightly before serving.

Vanilla Bean Cupcakes

Ingredients

- **1 cup** all-purpose flour
- **½ cup** sugar
- **½ tsp** baking powder
- **¼ tsp** baking soda
- **¼ tsp** salt
- **¼ cup** unsalted butter, softened
- **1 large egg**
- **½ cup** milk
- **1 tsp** vanilla bean paste (or extract)

Instructions

1. **Preheat Oven**: Preheat to 350°F (175°C) and line a cupcake tin with liners.
2. **Mix Dry Ingredients**: In a bowl, whisk flour, sugar, baking powder, baking soda, and salt.
3. **Combine Wet Ingredients**: In another bowl, cream butter and add egg, milk, and vanilla. Mix until smooth.
4. **Combine and Bake**: Gradually add dry ingredients to wet. Fill cupcake liners and bake for 15-18 minutes. Cool before frosting.

Enjoy your delicious treats!

www.ingramcontent.com/pod-product-compliance
Lightning Source LLC
LaVergne TN
LVHW081503060526
838201LV00056BA/2913